The 1

1

The Manager's view

I am aged 43.

I am a Store Manager.

I work in a furniture and carpet store.

It is called Carter's.

We are interviewing five people for a job this week.

The interviews are on Thursday morning.

The job is Assistant Store Manager.

Carter's is an out-of-town store.

We used to be in the town centre.

Now we are on the Park Road Estate.

We are next door to Asda.

Carter's have five stores.

Park Road is not the biggest.

Barnfield is the biggest store.

It is the Head Office.

Carter's is a private firm.

Two of the Carter family
still work here.

The Chairman is Tom Carter.

His nephew is a Store Manager.

He's not very good at his job.

He often gets things wrong.

About twenty people work at the Park Road store.

Some of them are part-time.

The store is open seven days a week.

From Monday to Saturday, we are open until 8 p.m.

On Sundays, we open from 10 a.m. until 4 p.m.

I need a good Assistant Manager.

The last one was O.K.

But he was only here for about a year.

He got a job with IKEA.

It is going to be difficult on Thursday.

We have to get it right this time.